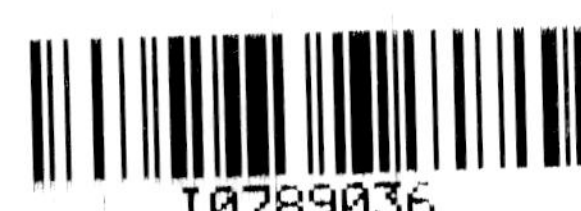

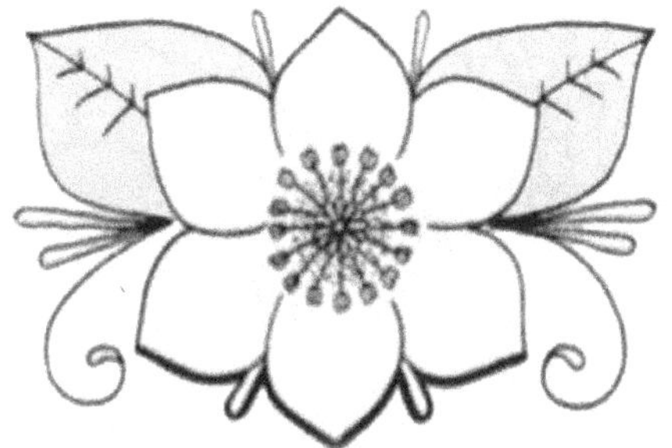

This Book Belongs To

____

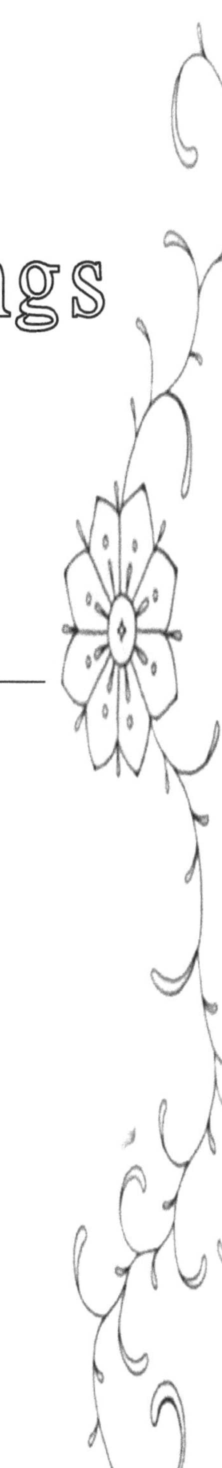

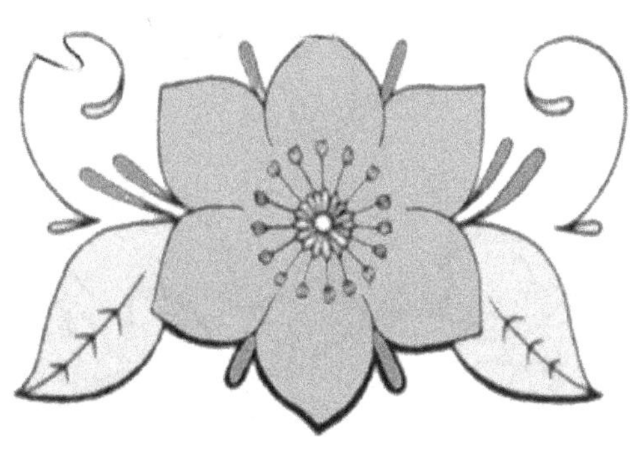

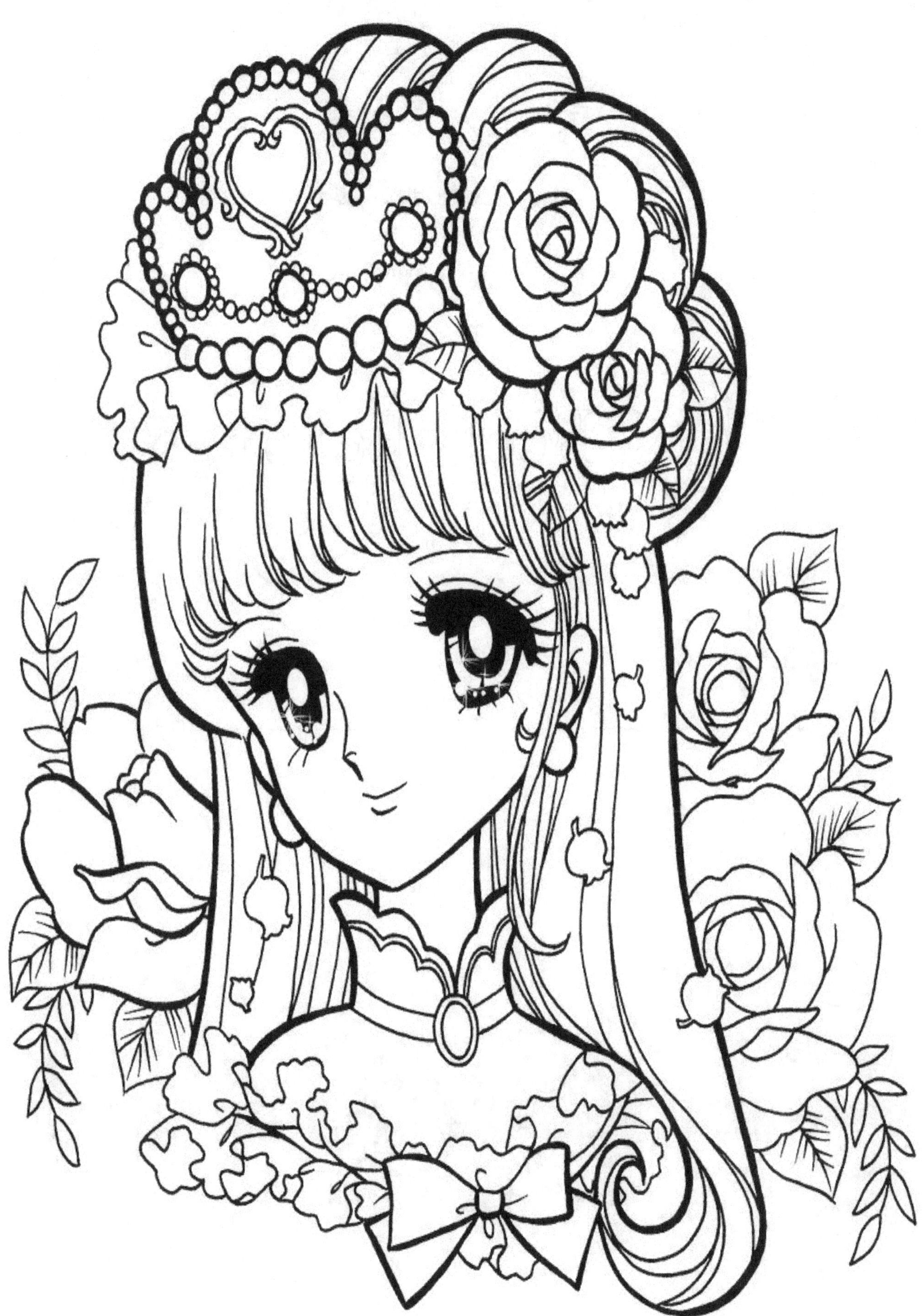

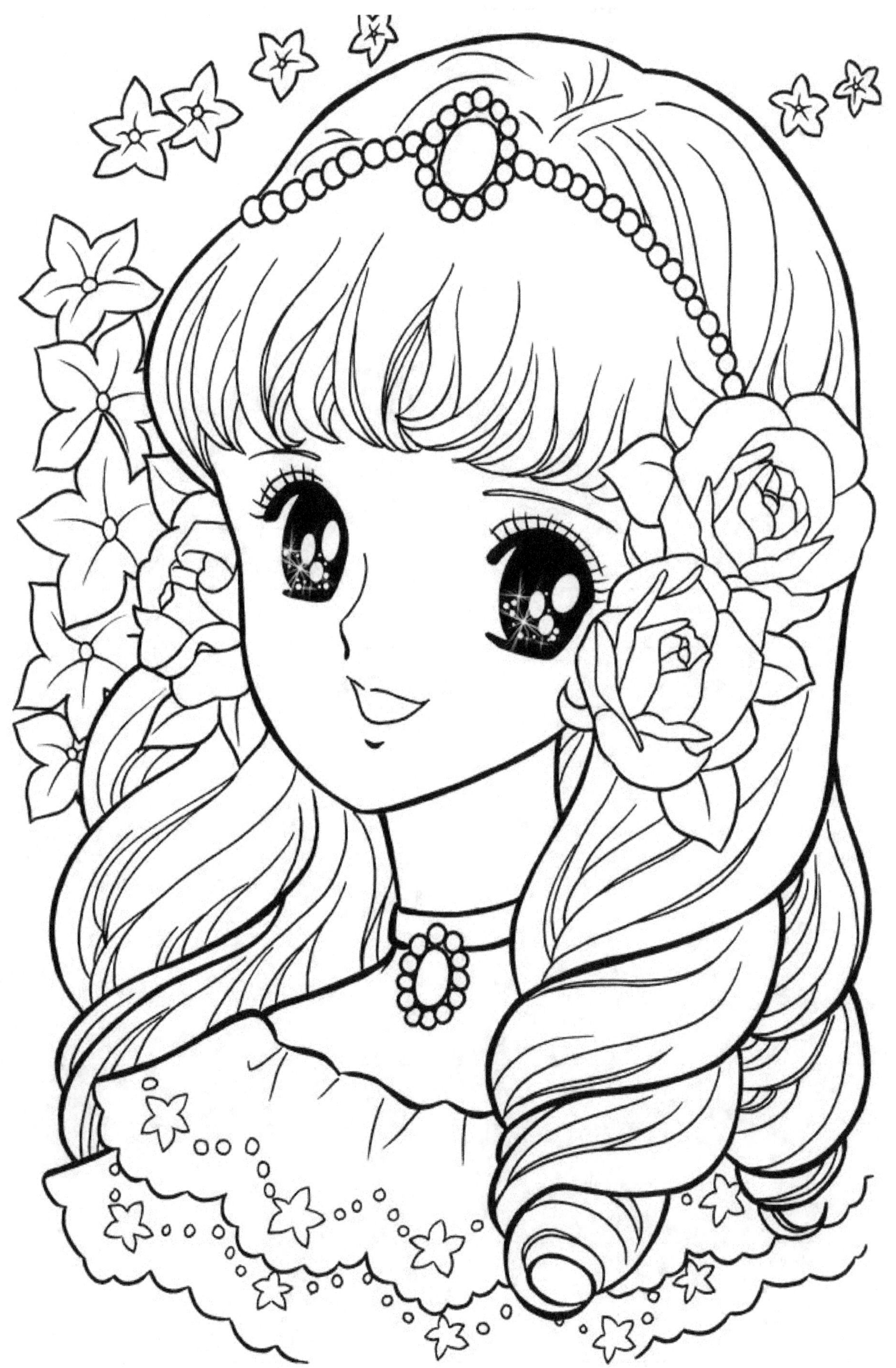

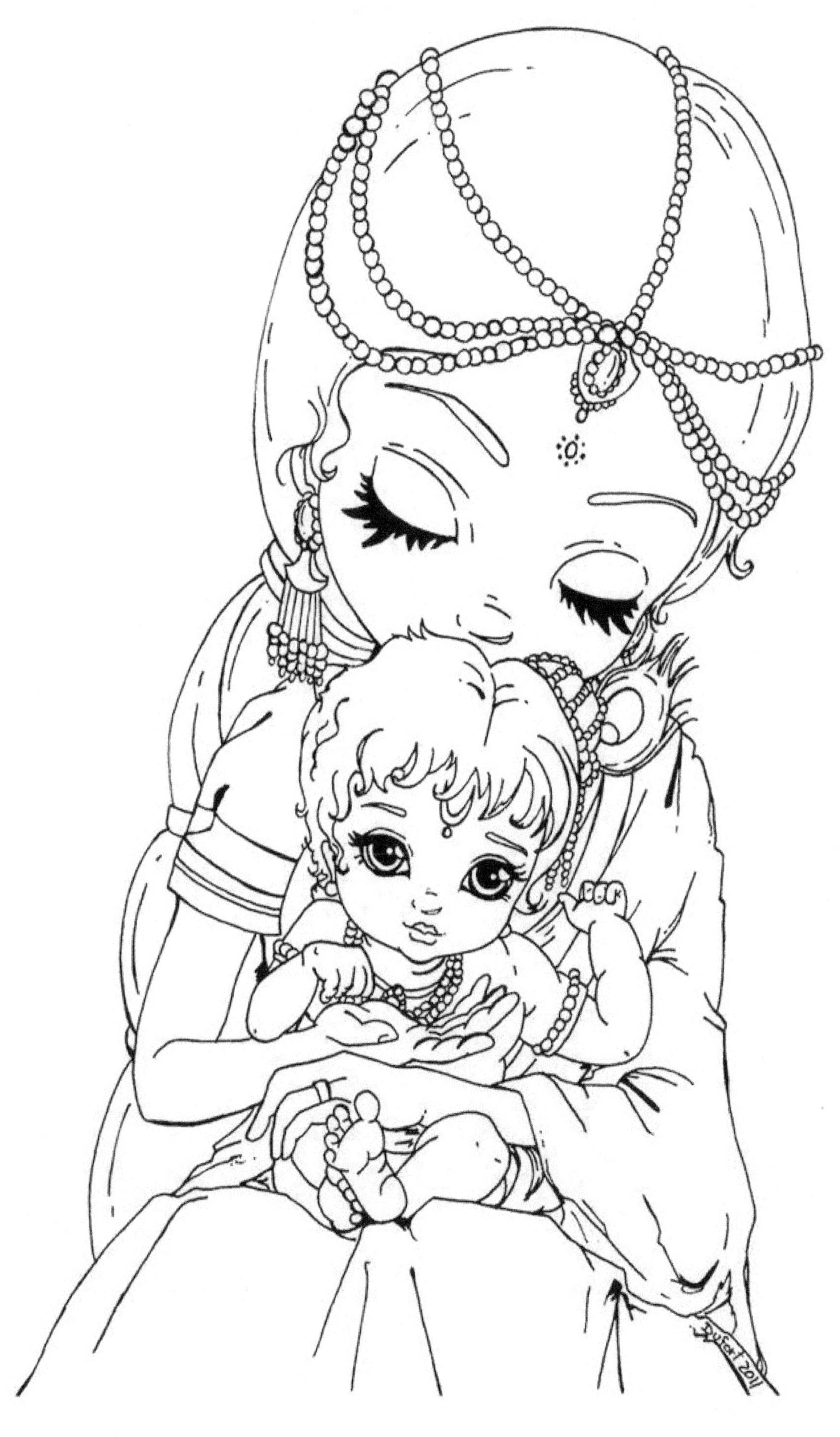

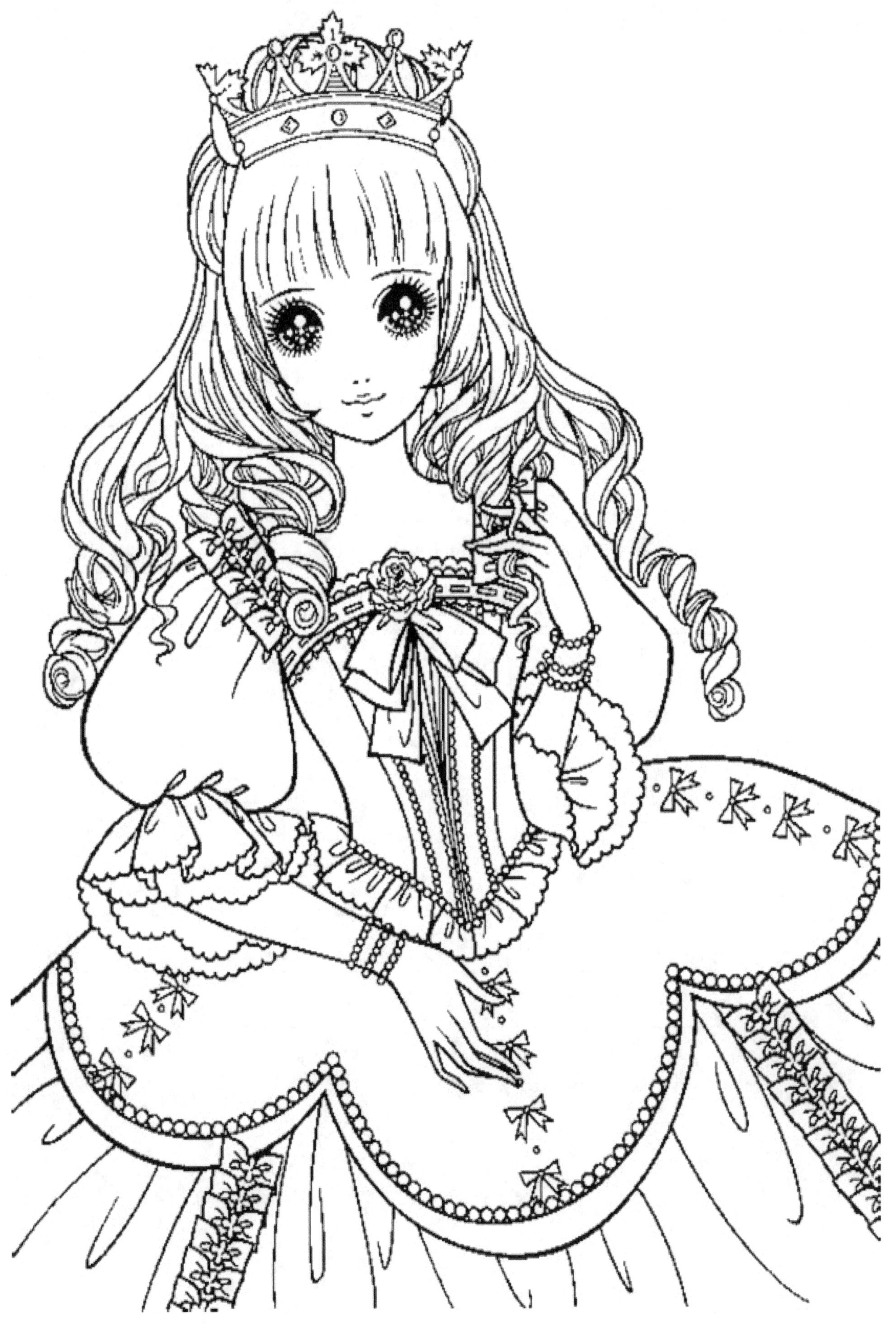

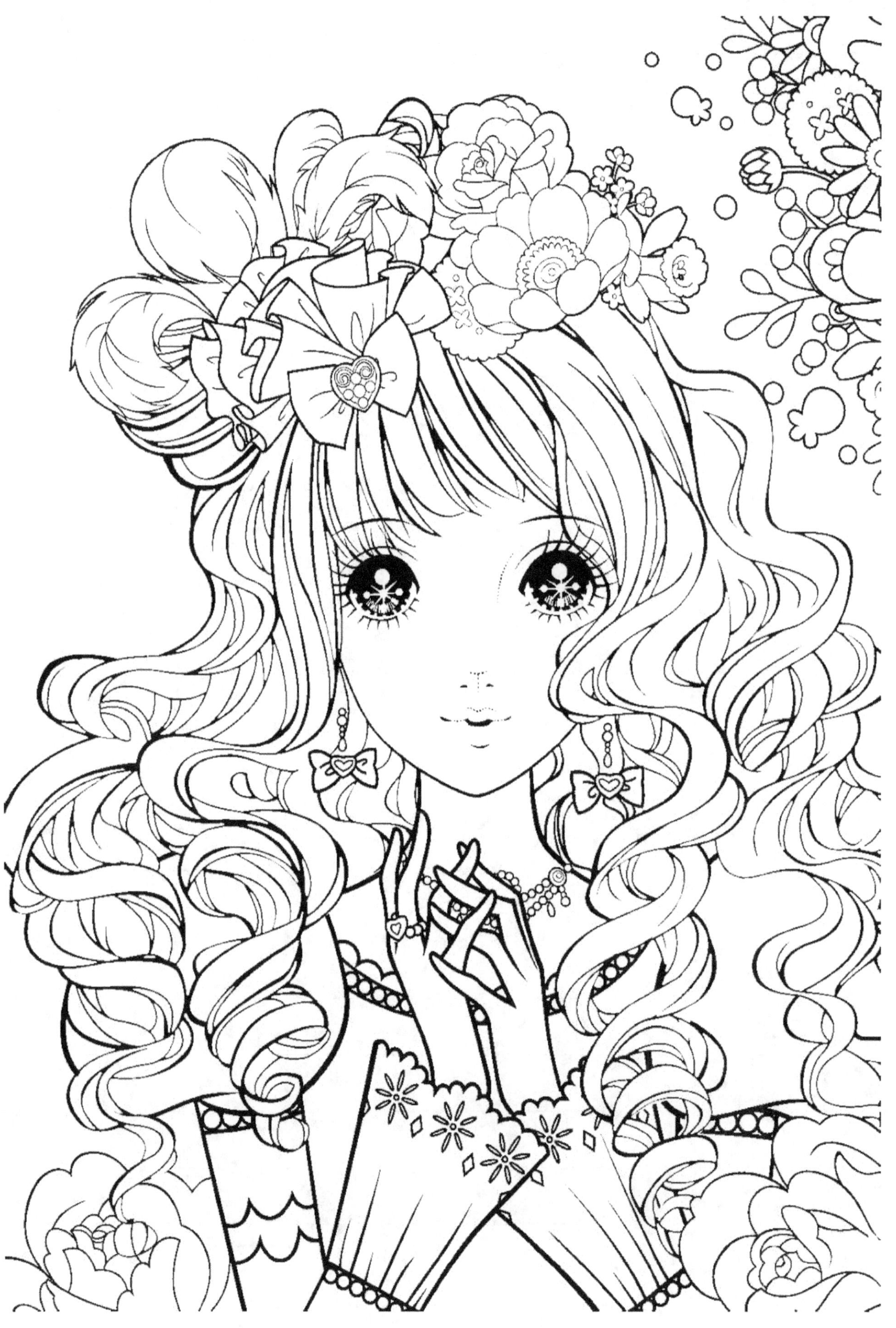

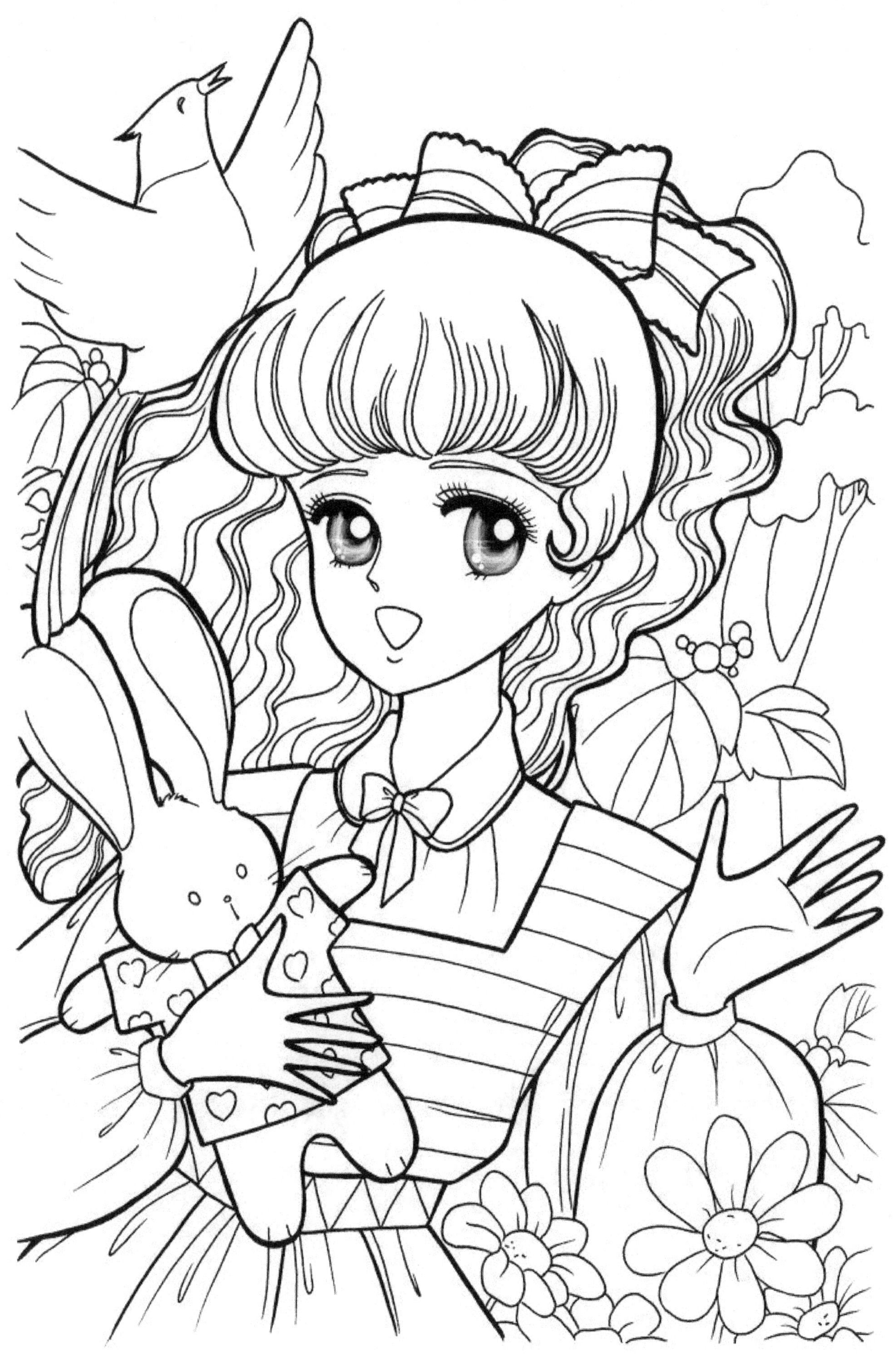

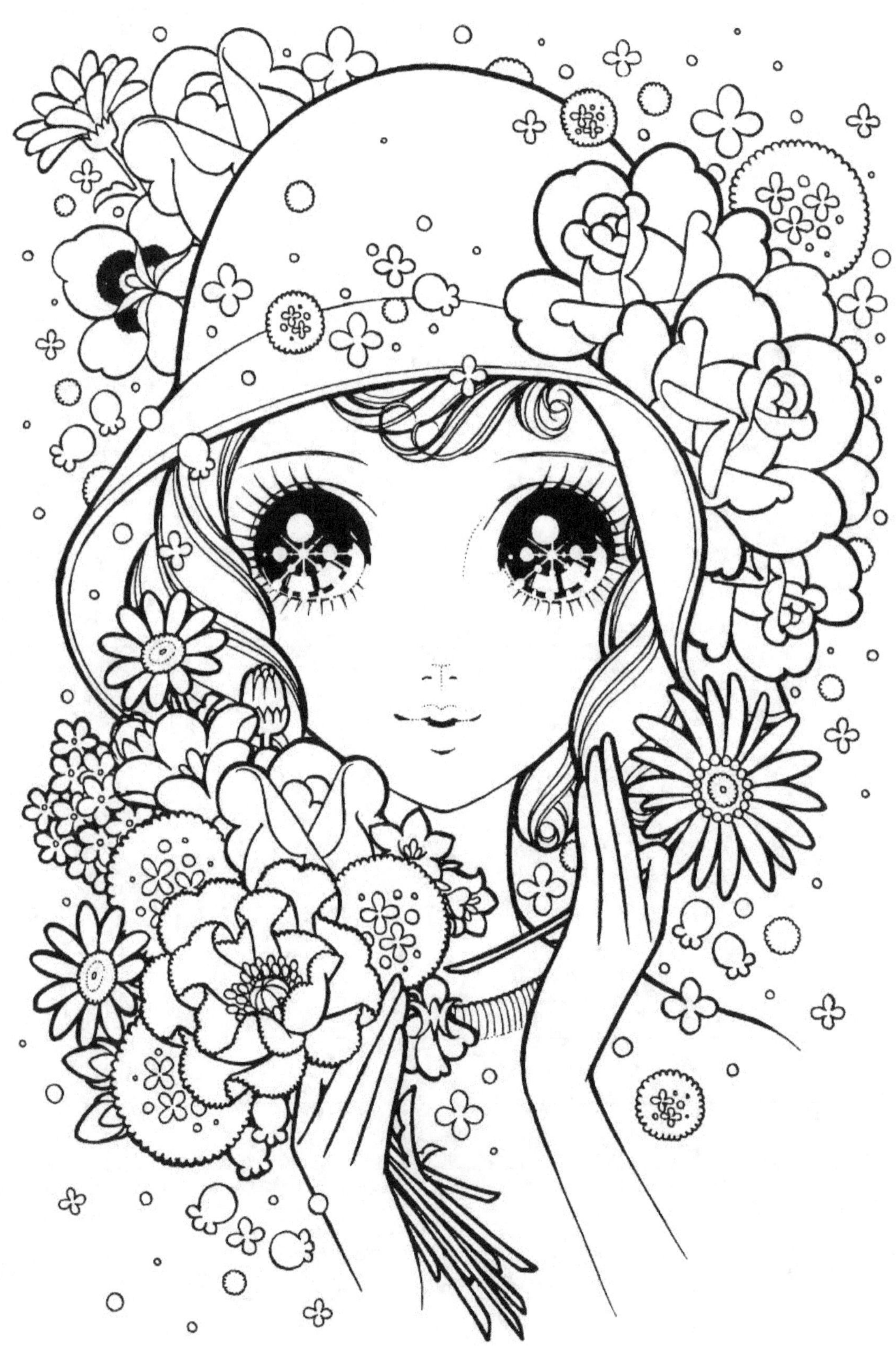

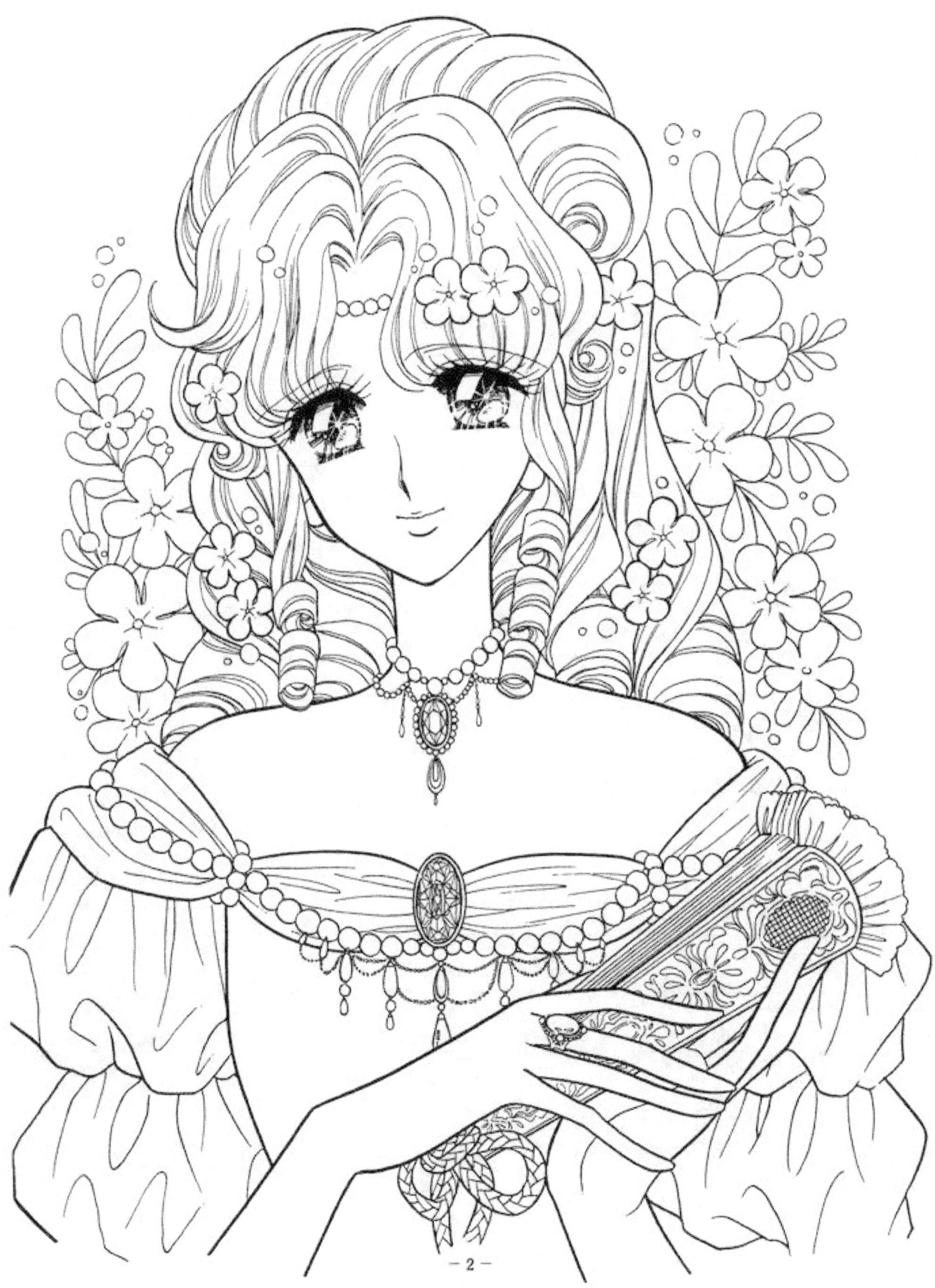

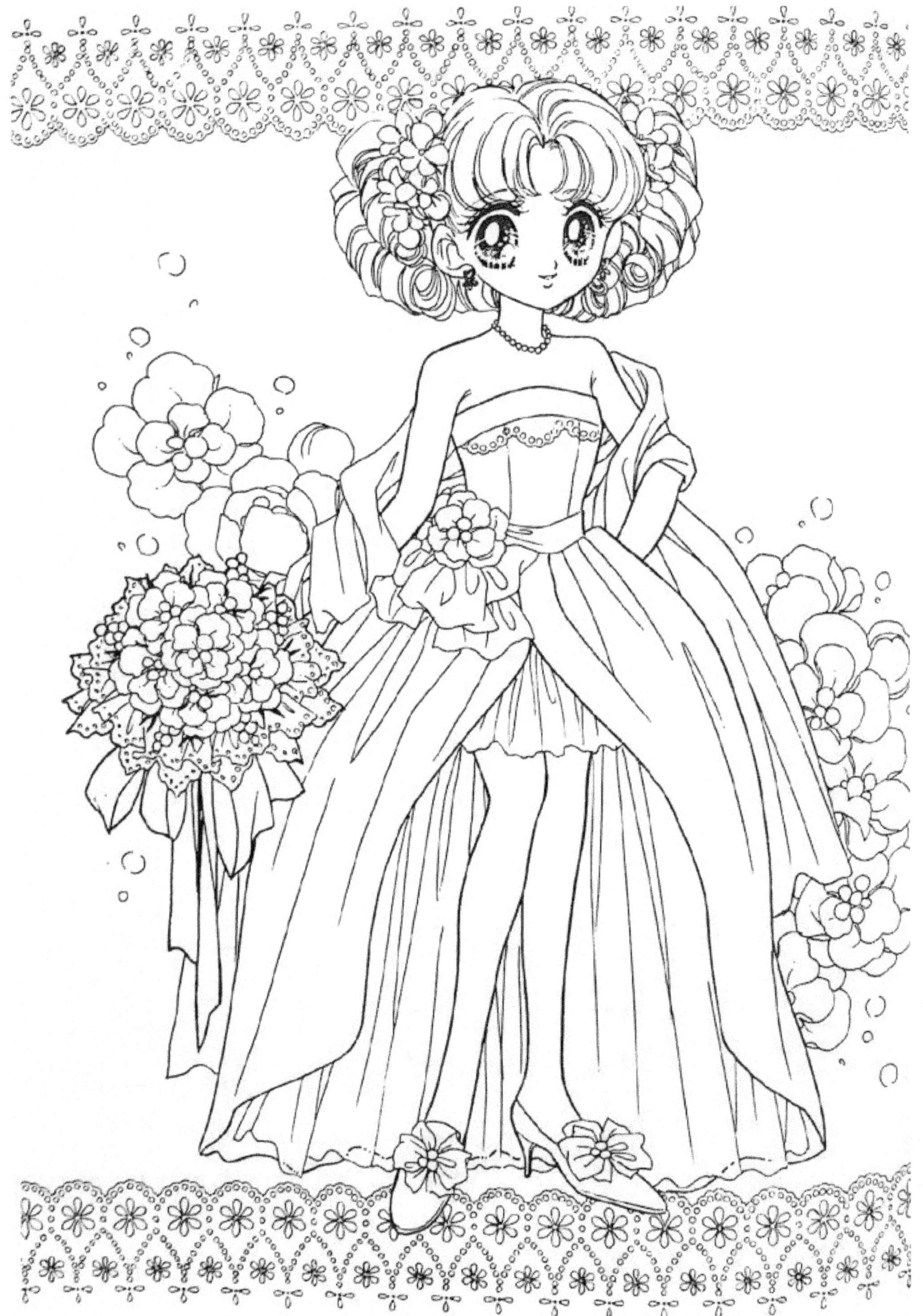

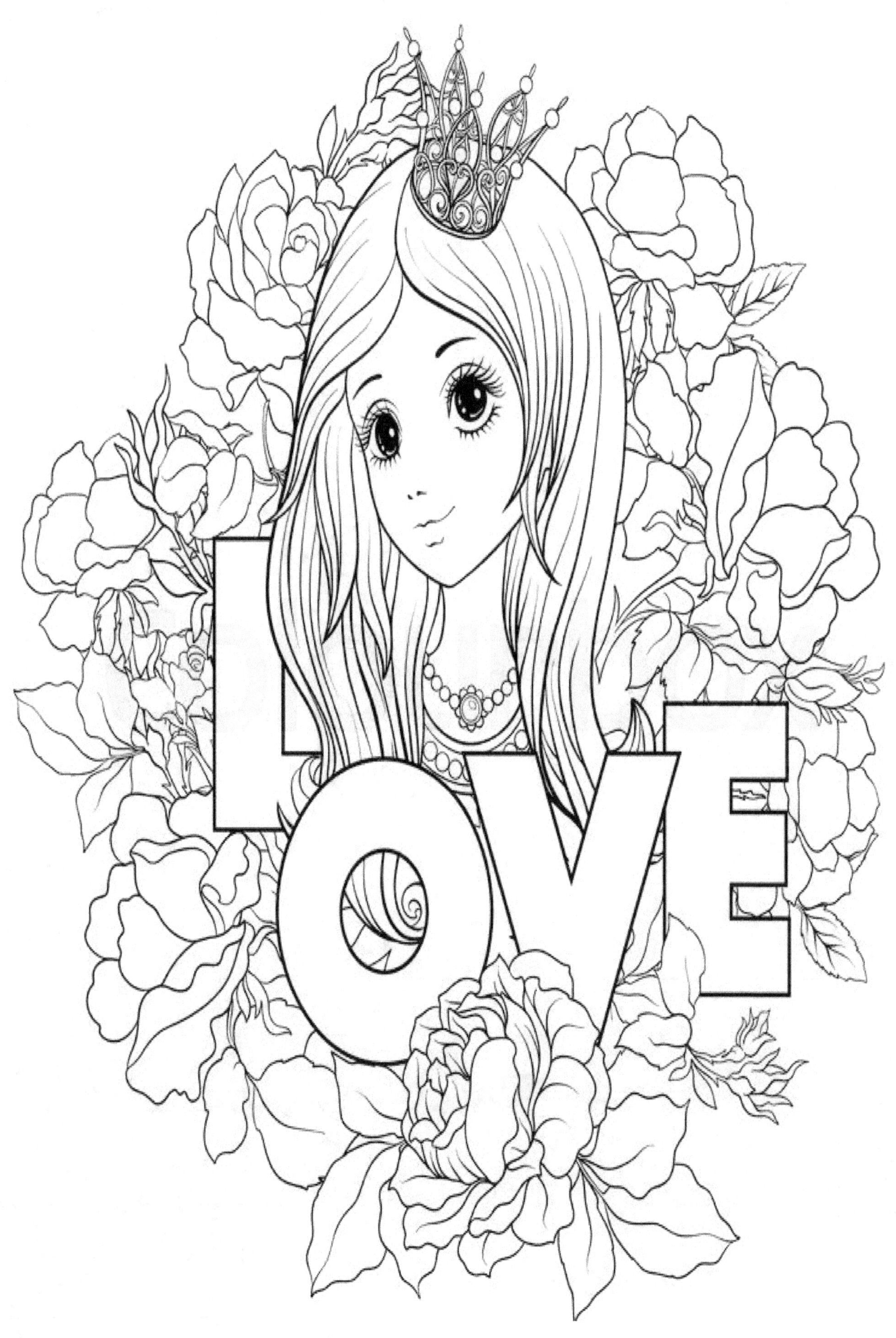

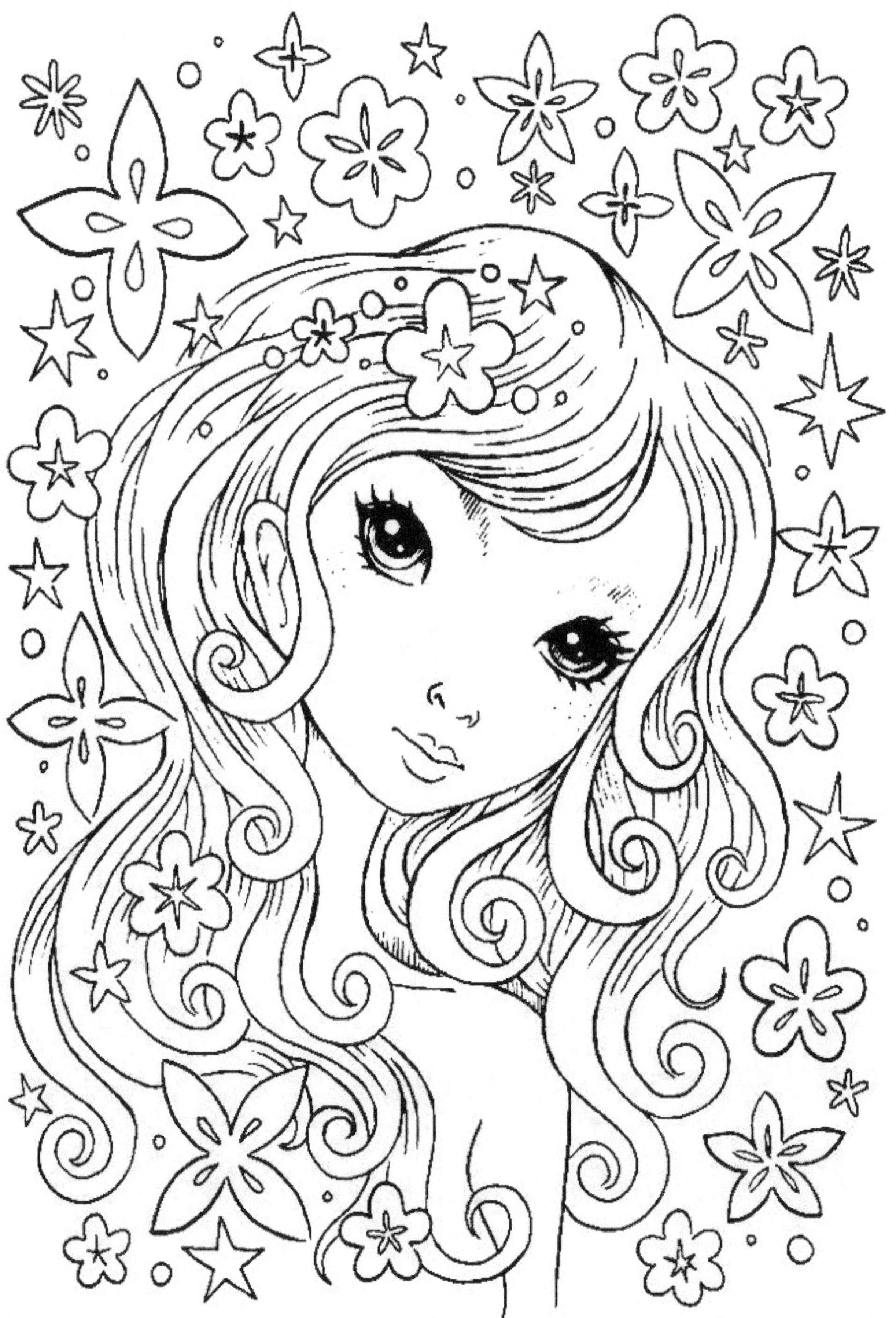

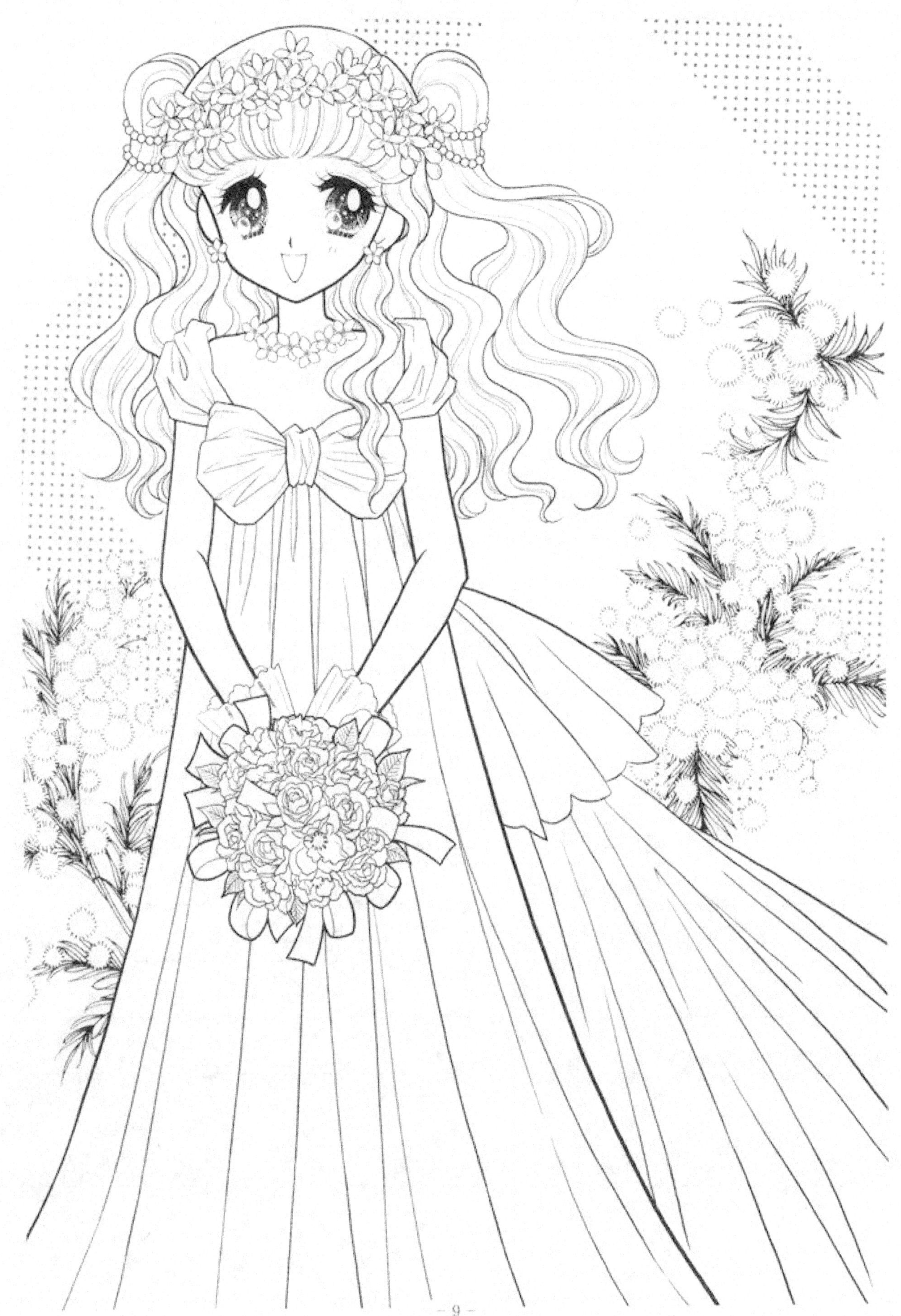

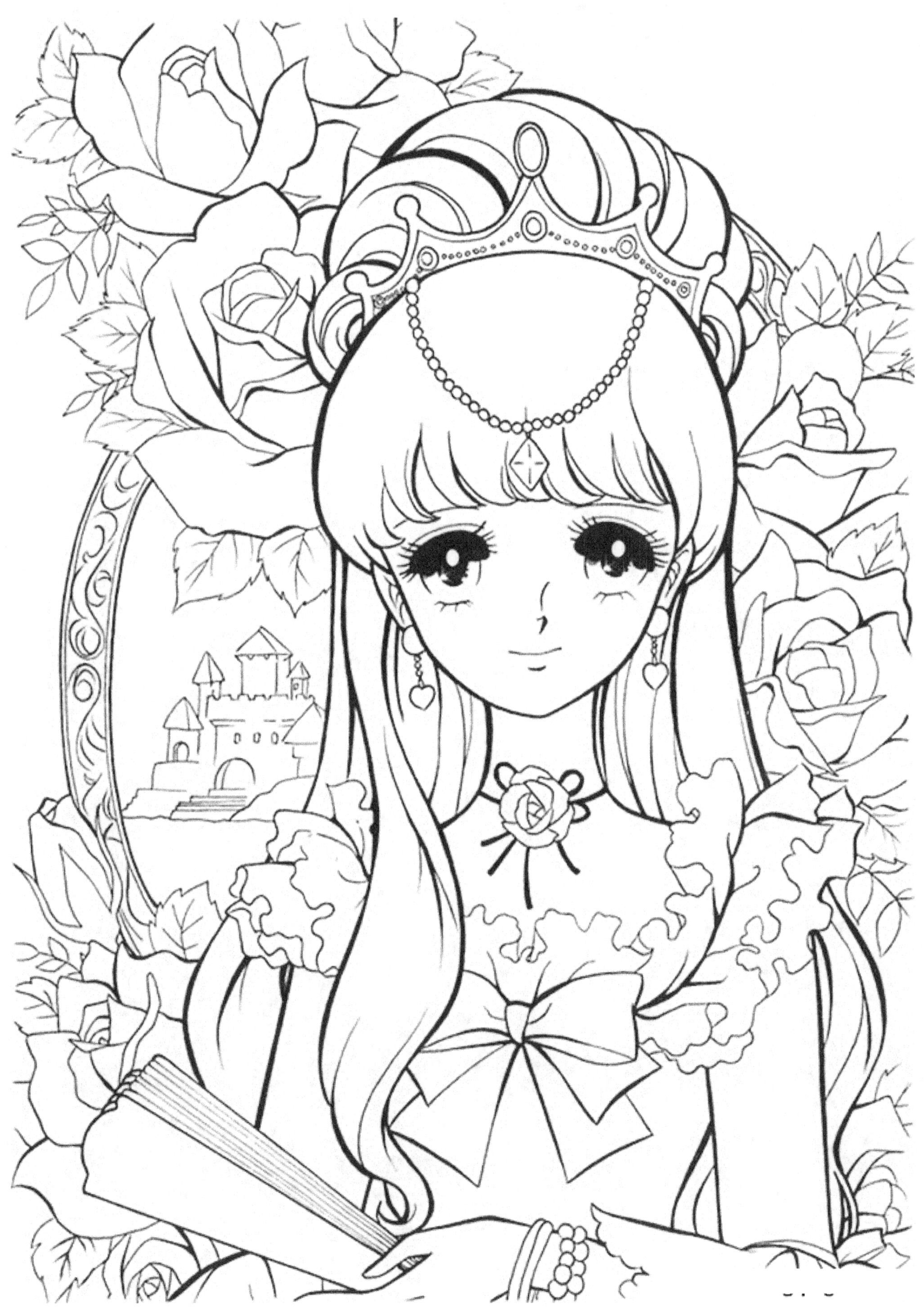

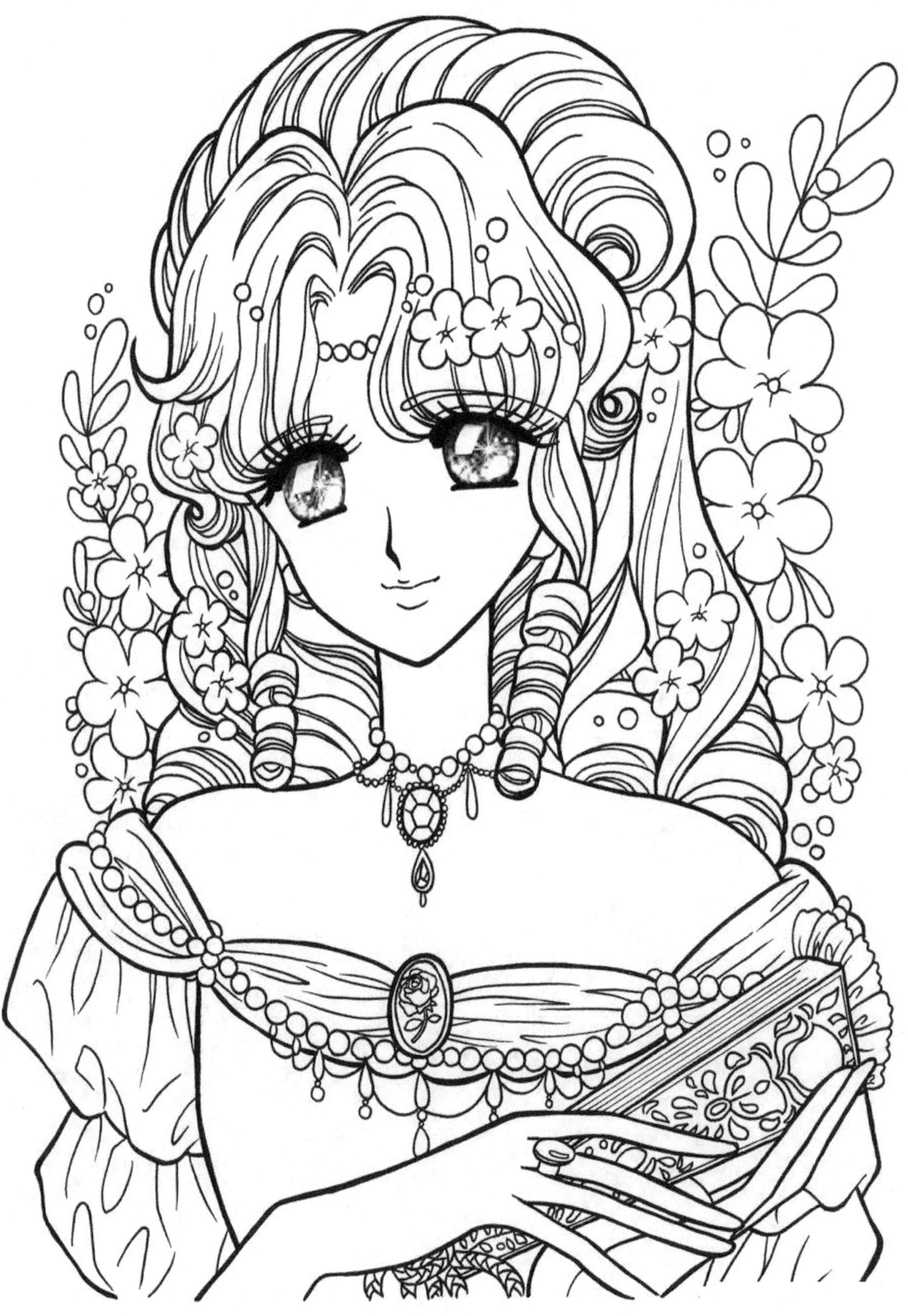

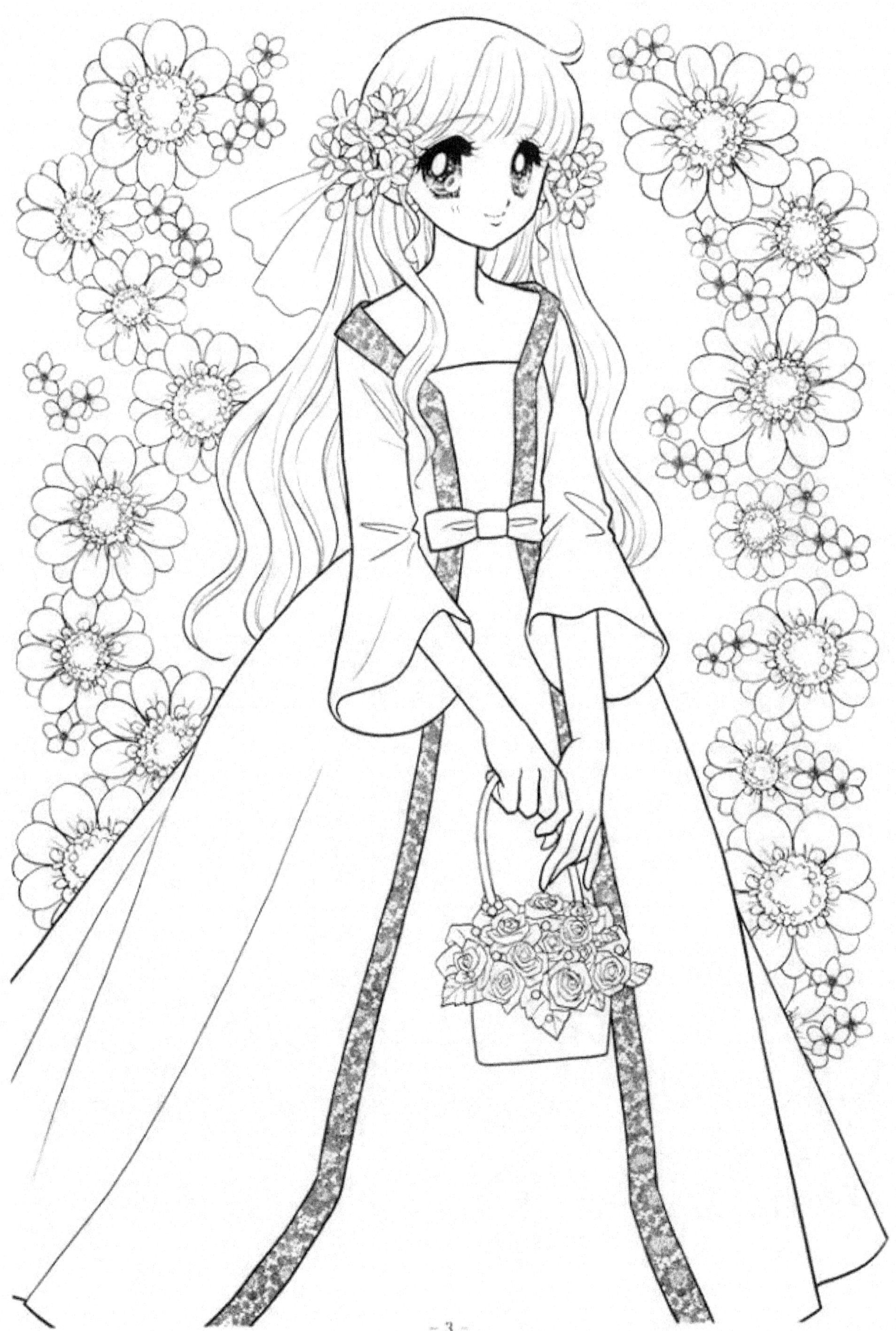

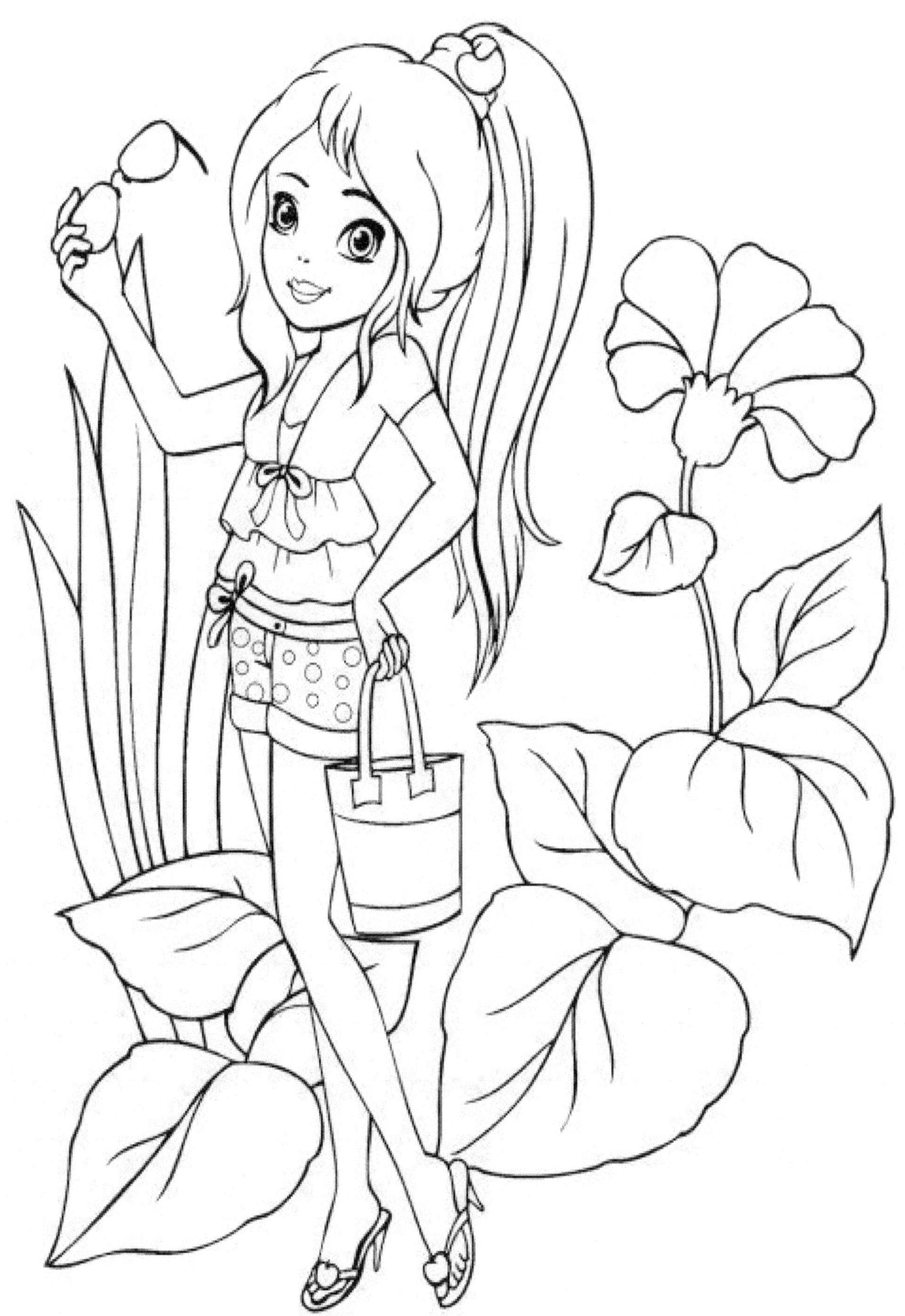

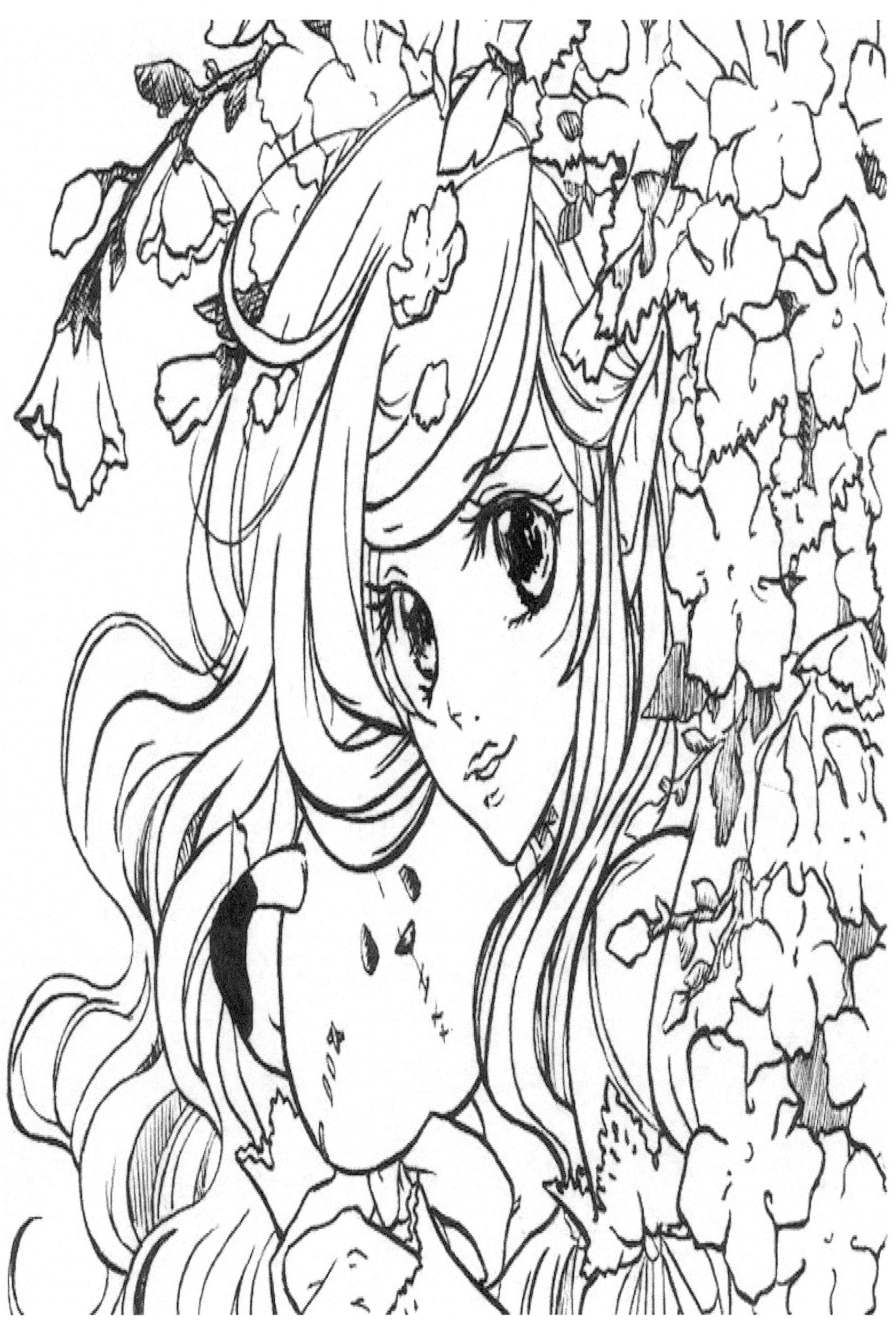

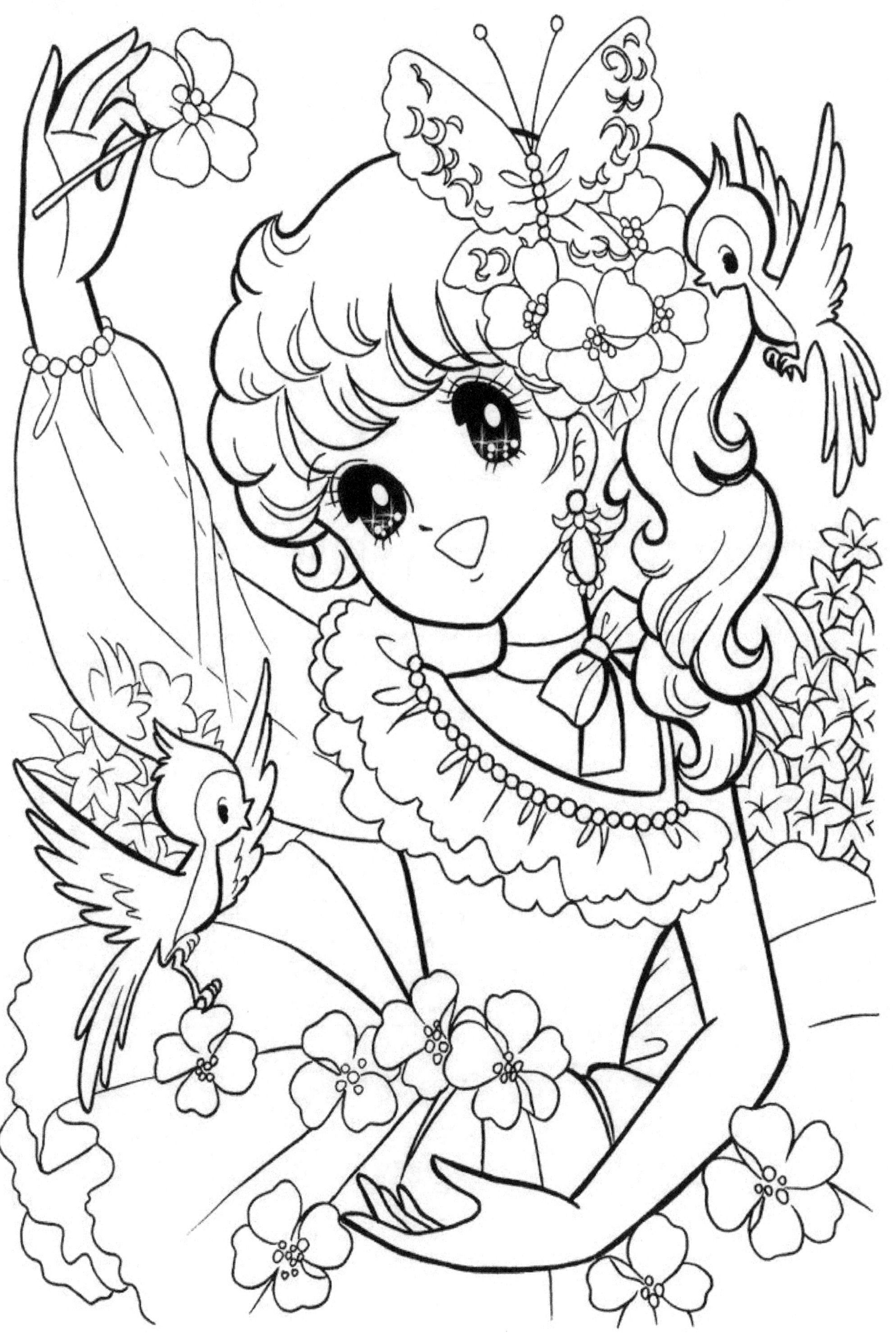

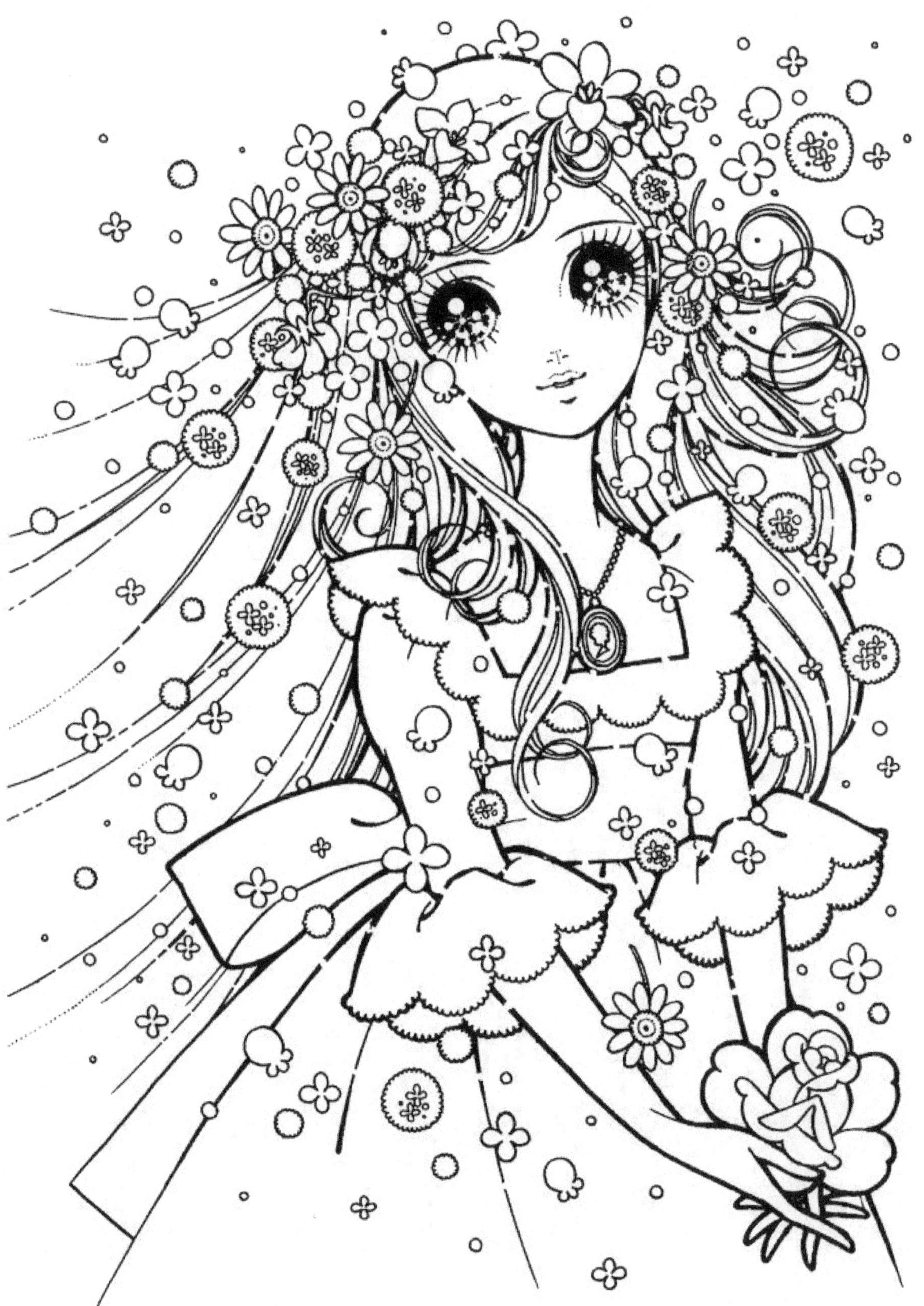

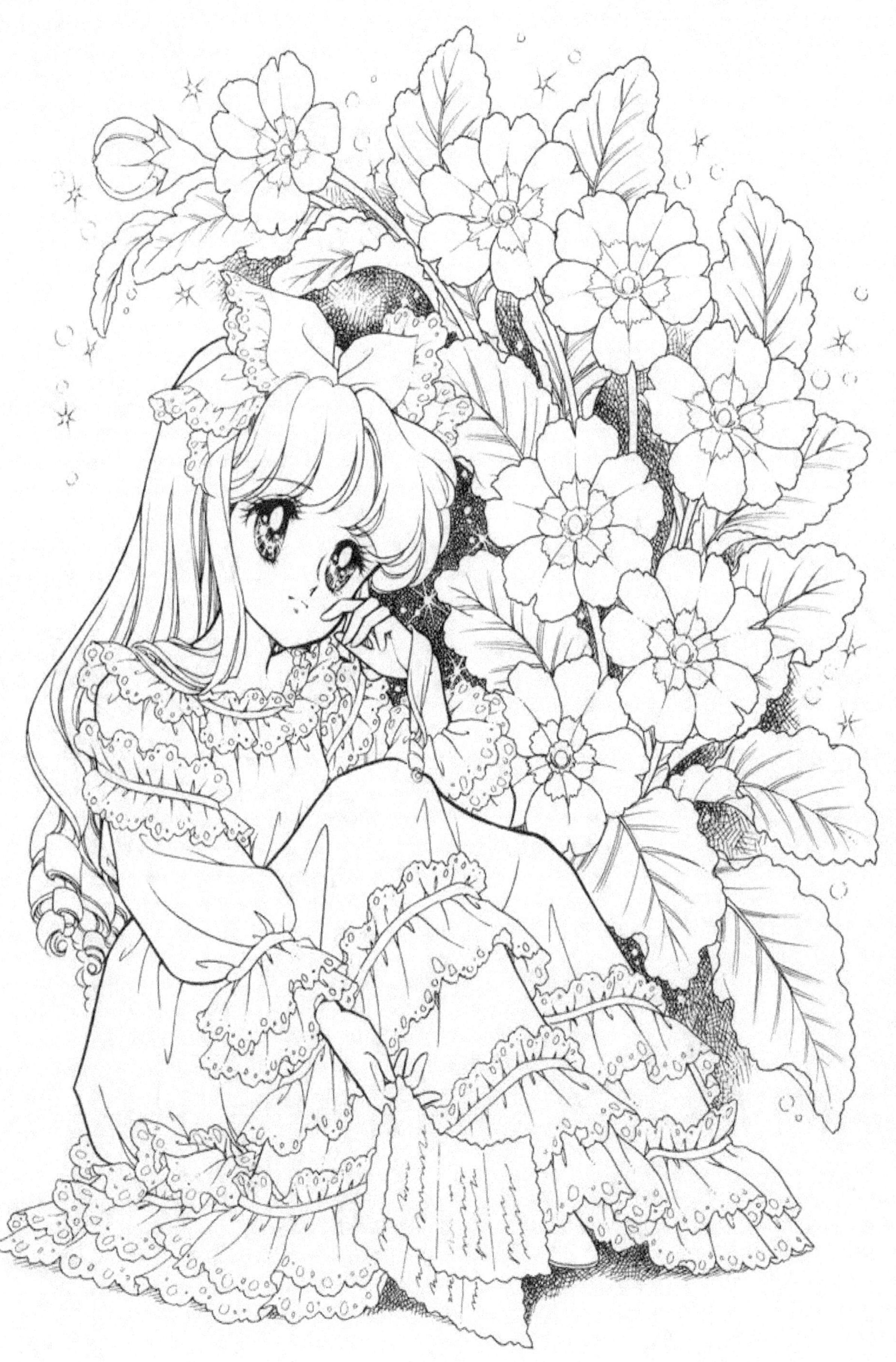

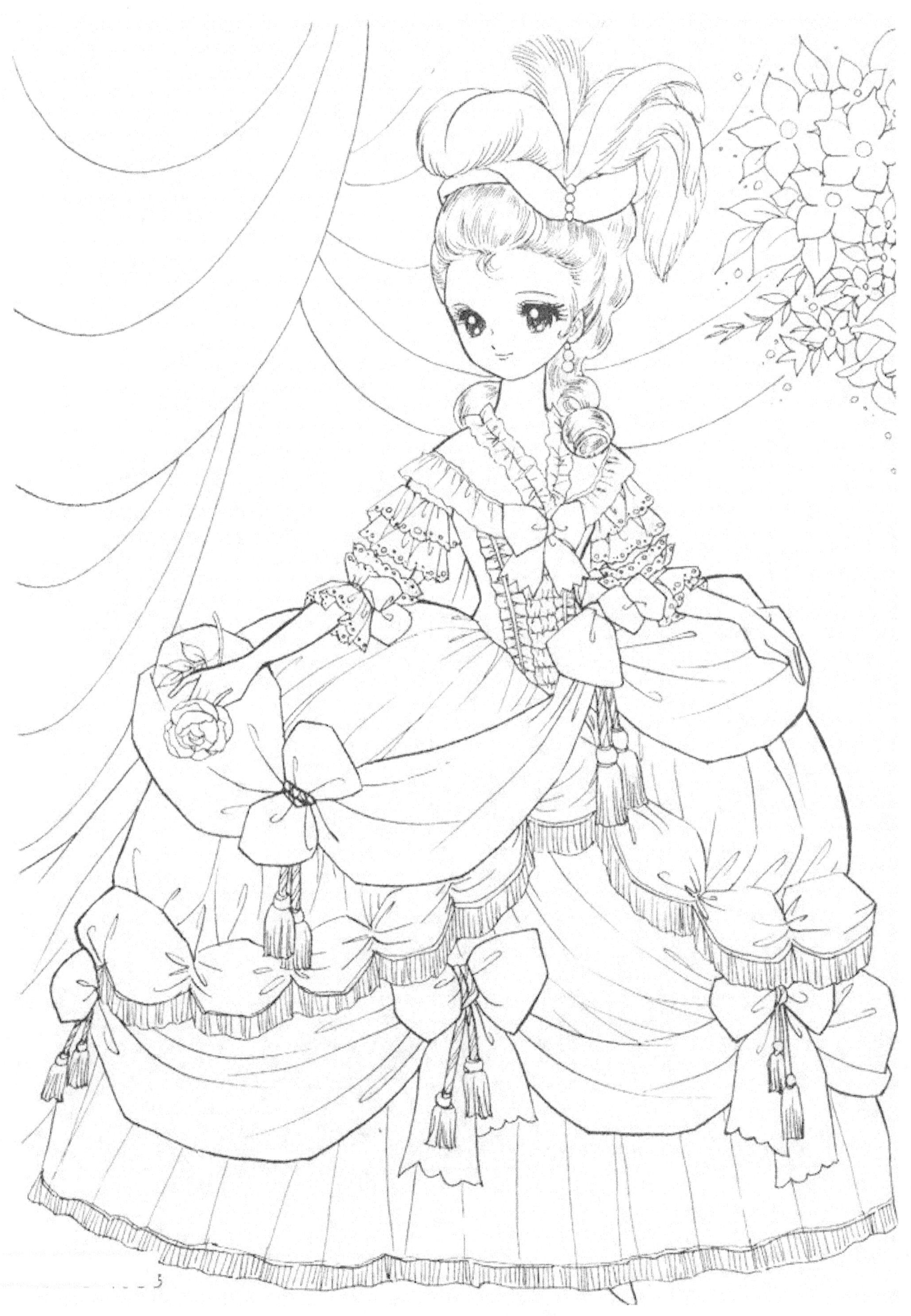

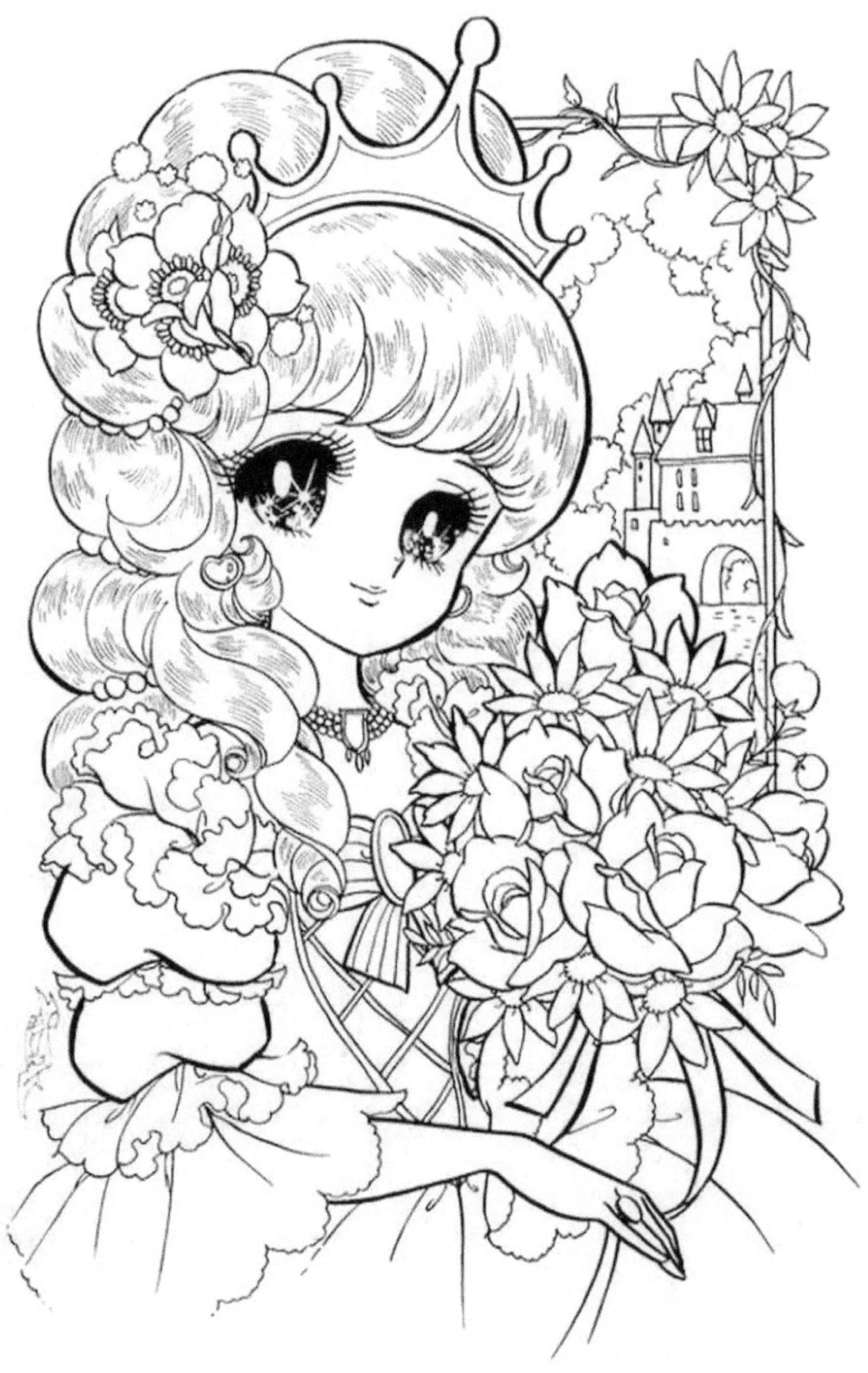

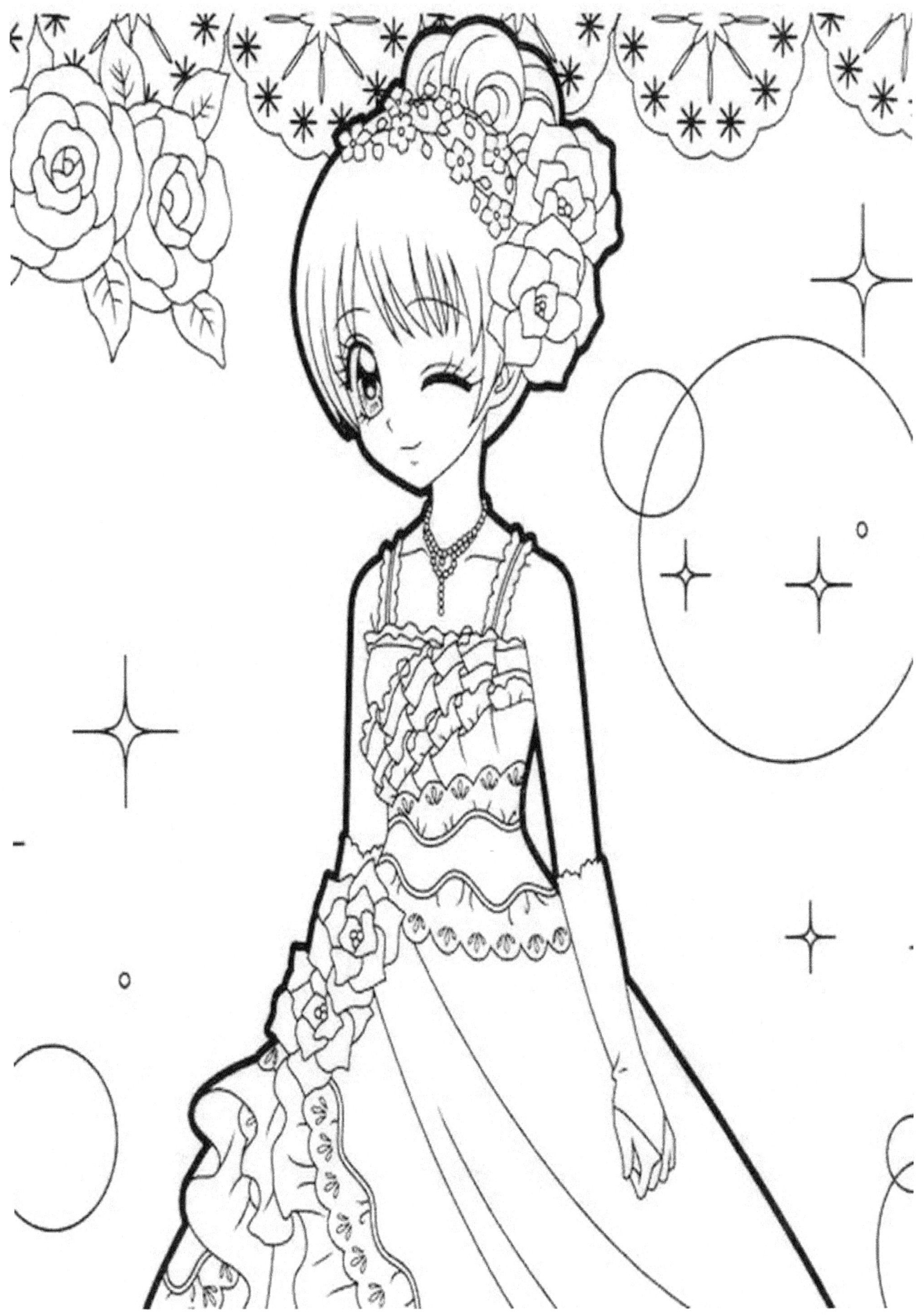

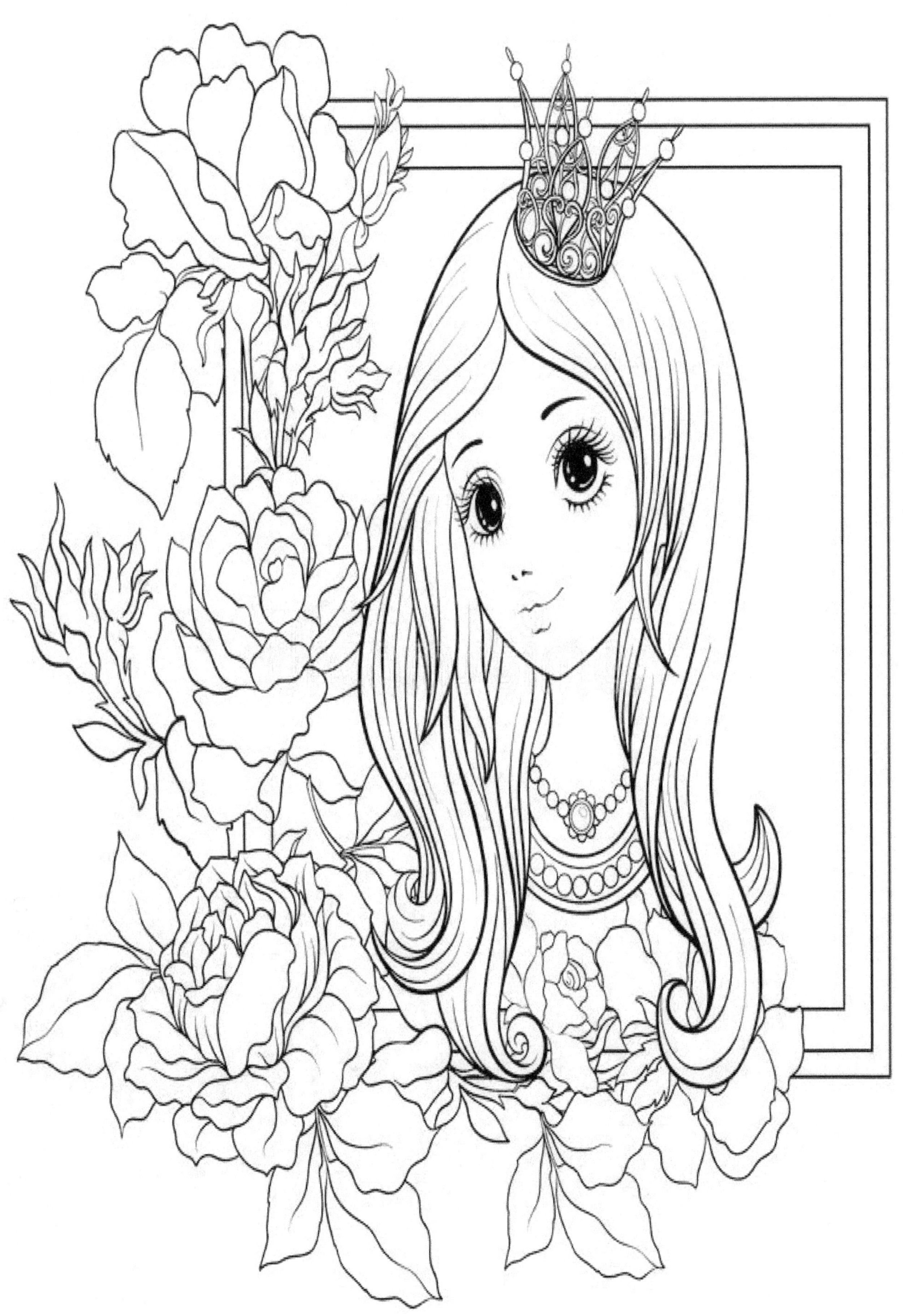

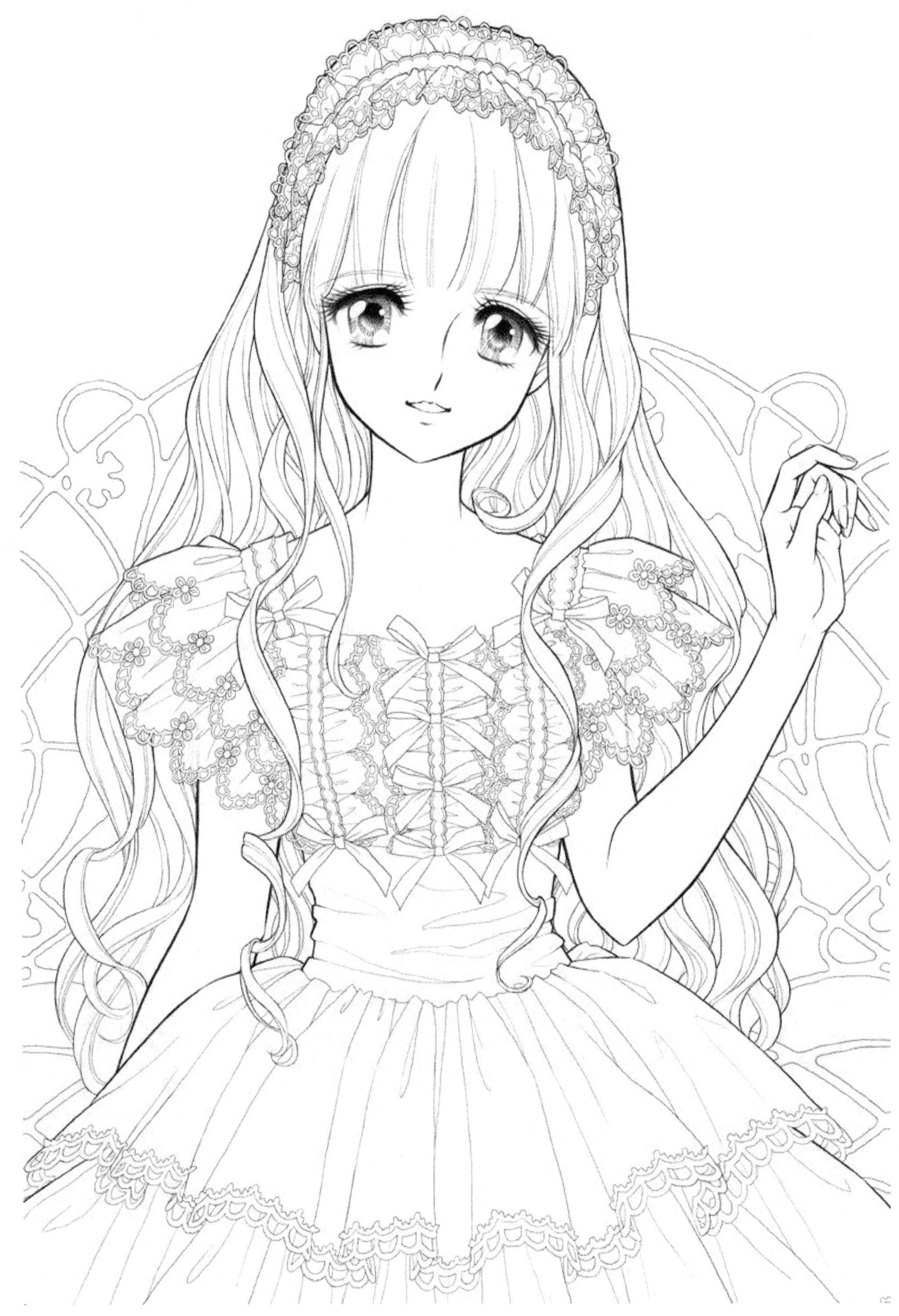